Gestation

Patricia Debney

Shearsman Books

First published in the United Kingdom in 2014 by
Shearsman Books
50 Westons Hill Drive
Emersons Green
Bristol
BS16 7DF

www.shearsman.com

ISBN 978-1-84861-366-9

THE SHEARSMAN CHAPBOOK SERIES, 2014

Martyn Crucefix *The Time We Turned*
Patricia Debney *Gestation*
juli Jana *ra-t*
Anthony Rudolf *Go into the Question*
Robert Vas Dias *Arrivals and Departures*

Contents

one

you

ask

you

        ask

I

        listen

you ask

I listen

you listen

        my heart

my heart

        hums in the distance

your voice

        tries every way in

        melts
        blends

this viscous

red pillow

answers

deep inside

I never recognise

your voice

two

so

long

on

my

own

and somewhere

      begins

the point when

      you know me

a lifetime after

      I dig in

hermit crab

      to your shell

out of

or with-

in

I grow

without you

three

you run up

                flights of stairs
at grad school

                double over
lose breath

the fact of the matter

                crushing you

do I conflate

          misrepresent

certainly I project

          yet

it is your telling

          remember

I am a curled over

                              fern frond

white as mushroom

                              sliced into

four

here

           I am

here

when does

another voice

speak to you

and is it

mine

my father

        rapes you

I think I see the house

        white walls
        formica table

        Bach
        Bob Dylan

you are that

        wide open

the billboard moves

       radio reaches out
       lashed to aluminium

I wait   buffeted
              buffered
              baffled

no one knows
I already have eyes and ears

my veins so close to the surface

              transparent

the body grows
what the body grows

I am root vegetable
in rich soil

rain falls
a kind of sun shines

and I push past
the first feeble skin:

shed like dust brushed
away, blown glass

you

                  lose your sense of touch

bruise

                  your whole left side

except for my

                  lump
                          bump
                                  rock hard

centre

I keep you here

years

six

I might be
                the dreams
                you had

or mine:

                those babies
                chicken skin folds
                enormous eyes

                somehow able to stand
                pull chairs to the cupboard
                open the door

                get out all the dead ones

                pickled in jars

somehow

        I don't die

and you

        survive

read me

        War and Peace

leave out

       the war

unspoken

   chasm

     between word

        and action

by now
the lighthouse calls

       safe passage
       new land

and beyond, darkness

       your studies
       job

       marriage

nothing can keep you
from landing this boat

except death
which you haven't (as far as I know)
tried yet

I am   your hope

salvation

  cosmic alignment

    truth from trees

  coded messages

    LSD

    music

dance

    me

I must tell you

I have never heard

your voices

eight

more of the same makes

tearing away

untangling

unravelling

loose ends

a bloody mess

and risk

       of your eclipse

                       grows

       only your outline

lit

sun

in

shadow

nine

now

I   fall

       land

              mostly on my feet

              like the cat

              you once rescued

              from the roof

       hit   the concrete

              and breathed

you   take flight

      let loose

            childhood balloons

            rough ribbon red

            bright blue yellow

            cut from my wrist

you   close your eyes

      face the wall

      disappear

born old

           I get older

and you

don't

die

young